Online
Entertainment

Patricia D. Netzley

ReferencePoint
Press®

San Diego, CA

For more information, contact:
ReferencePoint Press, Inc.
PO Box 27779
San Diego, CA 92198
www.ReferencePointPress.com

LIBRARY OF CONGRESS CATALOGING-IN-PUBLICATION DATA

Names: Netzley, Patricia D., author.
Title: Online entertainment / by Patricia D. Netzley.
Description: San Diego, CA : ReferencePoint Press, Inc., 2017. | Series: Digital issues | Includes bibliographical references and index.
Identifiers: LCCN 2016021525 (print) | LCCN 2016027251 (ebook) | ISBN 9781601529862 (hardback) | ISBN 9781601529879 (eBook)
Subjects: LCSH: Internet games--Social aspects--Juvenile literature. | Internet pornography--Juvenile literature. | Entertainment computing--Social aspects--Juvenile literature. | Internet addiction--Juvenile literature.
Classification: LCC GV1469.17.S63 N48 2017 (print) | LCC GV1469.17.S63 (ebook) | DDC 790.20285--dc23
LC record available at https://lccn.loc.gov/2016021525

CONTENTS

The Nature of Online Entertainment

Online entertainment provides people around the world with a lot of enjoyment—but some worry it has become too prevalent a part of daily life. Fifteen-year-old Lana Gorlinski of Orange County, California, is one person who worries that constant access to online entertainment inhibits teens' social and personal development. "It is far too easy to adopt the 'Why put out actual effort to play the guitar when I could torrent a funny movie and enjoy myself just as much?' attitude that often seems to be a given," says Gorlinski. "Ask the typical teenager what they like to do in their free time and they'll spend a good 20 seconds reminding themselves that Twitter and Netflix are not legitimate hobbies and trying to improvise a less pathetic answer."[1]

More People, More Options

Indeed, the number of people who rely on the Internet for entertainment has increased steadily over the past several years. According to experts in digital marketing, Internet traffic related to online gaming, for example, nearly doubled between 2014 and 2016. In addition, whereas there were roughly 172 million digital video viewers in the United States at the end of 2010, by the end of 2015 this number had grown to more than 200 million. Experts predict it will reach more than 244 million by 2018.

The number of people who listen to audio content online has also grown. According to the Pew Research Center, the percentage of individuals in the United States who have listened to an audio podcast in the past month rose from 9 percent in 2008 to 17 percent in January 2015. (A podcast—whether audio or video—is typically a talk program that is part of a themed series.)

There are also more options for online entertainment than ever before. As Marcus Wohlsen, who writes about business and technology issues for *Wired* magazine, says: "From mainstream streaming services like Netflix, Hulu, and Amazon Instant Video to niche sites like Funny or Die to YouTube celebrities—to name just some of the options that fall under entertainment—the kinds of moving pictures available and the ways to consume them have never been greater."[2]

> "From mainstream streaming services like Netflix, Hulu, and Amazon Instant Video to niche sites like Funny or Die to YouTube celebrities—to name just some of the options that fall under entertainment—the kinds of moving pictures available and the ways to consume them have never been greater."[2]
>
> —Marcus Wohlsen of *Wired* magazine.

Demanding Consumers

Experts who have studied digital trends note that much of the appeal of online entertainment—whether music, videos, e-books, or other online content—lies in the instant gratification that characterizes the Internet. And once people come to expect immediate satisfaction from the Internet, they often become more demanding. Consequently, as the professional consulting firm PwC reports, when it comes to online entertainment, "Consumers want more flexibility and freedom . . . in when and how they consume. They don't want schedules—they want it on-demand."[3]

One of the most common ways to satisfy the world's online entertainment demands is via streaming, whereby Internet audio and video materials are delivered to a computer, television, or other device in real time as a steady flow of data. Netflix and

A viewer uses an iPad connected to the video streaming service Netflix to watch the movie Avatar. Video streaming is one of the most common means of satisfying the world's online entertainment demands.

YouTube are among the most popular sites to offer streamed video content. As of 2016 Netflix had more than 75 million subscribers to its services in more than 190 countries, and surveys have shown that roughly 80 percent of teenagers and young adults who go online use YouTube, most commonly to view comedic, how-to, educational, and music videos.

Music can also be streamed via subscription services like Spotify and Pandora, and as with many aspects of online entertainment, the use of such sites has increased in recent years. For example, according to the International Federation of the Phonographic Industry (IFPI), an organization that represents recording companies, between 2010 and 2014 the number of people subscribing to such music services rose from 8 million to 41 million. Still, downloading songs remains more popular than streaming them, providing more than half of all digital revenue for music companies.

More Entertainment, More Problems

Since downloading transfers digital data onto a computer or other device in a way that allows the content to be stored for later viewing, downloaded songs and videos can be shared with others. But copyright laws make it illegal to copy, reproduce, or resell downloaded material without getting permission from the copyright holder to do so, or to download it in the first place without either gaining permission or paying for it. Nonetheless, many people see nothing wrong with illegally downloading or sharing songs and movies that have not been paid for.

According to a 2015 study by the independent media research organization Screen Audience Research Australia (SARA), 20 percent of people illegally download online content—an activity commonly known as pirating—simply because they can do it for free. Indeed, experts say it is relatively easy to steal via downloading. As Australian online entertainment experts Dave Court and Annie Parnell note: "Beginning about 20 years ago, the Internet placed almost the entirety of human creation in an unguarded window display and said, in effect, help yourself. The public, presented with an amazing smorgasboard of content, plunged right in."[4]

But gorging on Internet content is not always good for the consumer. Besides facing legal consequences due to piracy, downloads can result in the unintentional acquisition of malicious software and computer viruses. Engaging in indiscriminate Internet browsing can also lead to accidental views of pornographic and/or graphically violent media. Spending too much time online can lead certain users to develop a dependency on the Internet that some experts label an addiction. Such drawbacks, however, do not deter most people from increasingly turning to the Internet for entertainment. In fact, industry analysts predict that growth related to all forms of such entertainment will continue for years to come—and these forms of entertainment are one day likely to crowd out their offline counterparts.

> "Consumers want more flexibility and freedom . . . in when and how they consume."[3]
>
> —Professional consulting firm PwC.

CHAPTER ONE

How the Internet Has Affected Entertainment Providers

In the days before the Internet, writers, filmmakers, musicians, and other artists who wanted to reach large audiences typically had no choice but to go through "gatekeepers"—the people who control major motion picture, television, music, and publishing companies. That is, artists had to sell their work to corporate representatives first and foremost. Music industry expert Jeff Price explains how this worked in the record business:

> It used to be that as a musician, you had to go to the "artist gatekeeper," the [record] label, and be one of the anointed few that got the privilege of transferring ownership of what you created to the label so your CDs could end up on store shelves. In order to get heard, and then hopefully have your music cause a reaction, you had to be one of the even luckier few chosen by the "consumer gatekeepers" to have your music played on commercial radio or MTV, or get written about in *Rolling Stone* [magazine].[5]

Far too often, such representatives cared more about the name of the artist than about the quality of the work. This meant that a poorly performed song or a badly written novel by someone famous had a much greater chance of reaching consumers than an excellent work by an unknown. The Internet, however, presents a different route to success. As Price says, thanks to the Internet, "the general population of the world can decide what does and does not have value, and can share thoughts and preferences in scales never before thought imaginable, networking to one another globally, via social outlets like Twitter, FaceBook, MySpace, and YouTube."[6] Consequently, it is possible for individuals with no connections and little money to acquire fame, and possibly wealth, simply by putting their creative works online.

A Way to Get Rich

Among the most prominent examples of someone who became wealthy as a result of sharing work online is famous singer/ songwriter Justin Bieber. In 2007, when he was an unknown twelve-year-old, his mother posted a video on YouTube of him performing in a singing competition. (He had placed second.) Friends and relatives responded so positively to the video that she decided to post several more on the site. Strangers also began to watch Bieber sing, and soon his videos were viewed millions of times. More significantly, a recording industry marketer saw one of the videos and asked Bieber to record some demo tapes for him. Shortly thereafter, the then-thirteen-year-old had a recording contract, and today he earns $60 to $80 million each year.

Another way to get rich from an online video has to do with the way sites like YouTube create income for those willing to share their clips. YouTube keeps the details of its profit sharing with its content providers a secret, but experts in online media do know that artists can share in the money made from advertisements on YouTube. These come in the form of either banner ads that that pop up while a video is playing or video clips that play before the selected YouTube offering.

One artist who has benefited from such revenues is the Korean pop star Psy. In 2014 the music video of his song "Gangnam Style" became the first YouTube video to hit 2 billion views, an

The South Korean singer Psy performs his hit song "Gangnam Style." The music video of "Gangnam Style" became the first video to hit 2 billion views on YouTube.

accomplishment that took less than two years. (At the time, the next most popular YouTube video was of Justin Bieber performing his song "Baby," at more than 1 billion views.) As a result, experts estimate, Psy earned nearly $2 million from YouTube ad views, as well as an additional $8 to $10 million from other sales related to his viral "Gangnam Style" YouTube video and online sales of the song via iTunes.

A Way to Become Famous—or Notorious

Psy was able to garner so many views in such a relatively short time because his video went viral, which means that viewers shared it often and rapidly via online posts and/or e-mail forwards. As Clint Rainey, a writer for *New York* magazine, reports, "In a matter of hours, a video can go viral and be viewed 50 million times."[7] It can also be collectively viewed for millions of hours. In fact, according to YouTube, its ten most viral moments of 2015 were watched for more than 25 million hours.

But not every viral video makes its subject wealthy. Sometimes it simply makes a person famous in a way that is sudden and unexpected. As Rainey notes, "Internet fame comes on like an earthquake, with little warning."[8] Based on his interviews with the subjects of viral videos, he says that some people are happy with this type of fame, while others have found it upsetting.

An example of a positive experience with a viral video is that of Judson Laipply. His six-minute YouTube video of a comic dance routine went viral in 2006, ultimately attracting more than 296 million views. He credits the resulting fame with allowing him to make a career out of dancing. In contrast, former beauty pageant contestant Caite Upton was left seriously depressed after a 2007 video of her being interviewed onstage at the Miss Teen USA pageant went viral. Viewed more than 64 million times, this video showed her flubbing an answer about maps and geography so badly that she became an instant object of ridicule. Not only was she verbally attacked in person and in messages, but her performance was mocked in other people's videos and video series.

> "In a matter of hours, a video can go viral and be viewed 50 million times."[7]
>
> —Clint Rainey of *New York* magazine.

Control over One's Experience

People in Upton's situation have no control over how the public will react to the videos shared online. The same is true of interactive events involving the public at large. For example, live question-and-answer sessions involving authors can easily lead to heckling because they are uncontrolled. This was the case with a June 2015 Twitter event for author E.L. James, whose novel *Fifty Shades of Grey* has explicit sexual content. Seija Rankin of Eonline.com reports: "The afternoon turned into a straight-up spectacle of circus proportions, with Twitter users firing anti-Fifty Shades of Grey zingers left and right."[9]

However, James did have control over her publishing experience, because she initially self-published her novel in 2011 as both an e-book (an electronic book downloaded off the Internet) and a print-on-demand paperback (a book printed after the order for it is received). She then used viral marketing techniques to spread interest in her book via social media websites. After this generated sufficient buzz, a traditional publisher rereleased the edition that now appears in bookstores.

Another example of an author who turned to self-publishing in order to gain greater control over his work is novelist Hugh Howey. In 2011 he turned down a traditional book contract from a small press so he could sell his post-apocalyptic thriller *Wool* online. After selling more than a thousand copies in just a few months, he released an expanded version of *Wool* in January 2012 known as the *Wool* omnibus. It soon landed on the *New York Times* e-book best-seller list in the fiction category, and by the middle of the year monthly sales had grown to between twenty thousand and thirty thousand copies, earning Howey $150,000 a month.

Hugh Howey, author of the novel Wool, *delivers hard copies of his book for shipping. Howey's novel became a best seller after he released an expanded version online.*

Howey is also notable for the way his actions expanded book contract options for authors. Specifically, his success attracted the attention of traditional publishers who offered him hundreds of thousands of dollars for the rights to publish print and digital versions of his omnibus, but he refused all of these offers until one publisher, Simon & Schuster, agreed to allow him to retain his digital rights. He thus became the first self-published author ever to be offered a print-only contract by a major publisher.

Based on his experiences, Howey believes that the publishing industry is adapting well to new developments in online entertainment. He explains:

> I think of all the industries that have been revolutionized by digital media, publishers have done a great job [of adapting]. They've gone from [stigmatizing] self-publishing to looking at the bestseller list to find people who aren't signed, snatching them up and giving them much fairer contracts, and embracing the fact that they can publish several books in a year and have this huge fan base they can bring with them.[10]

Fan Fiction

Indeed, the Internet makes it easy for fan bases to develop and grow, by uniting people from all over the world who enjoy the same types of entertainment. It also provides individuals who love a particular television show, movie, or novel with forums in which they can expand on beloved works via their own creative efforts. In some cases, this leads to entirely new works. In others, it leads to variations on existing works.

James's *Fifty Shades of Grey* is an example of a story that arose from the desire of a fan to create a new work based on a beloved one. Also known as fan fiction, this work is a type of fiction whereby fans employ the characters and/or settings from an original work of fiction in their own work, typically without the original author's permission. A huge fan of the *Twilight* book series by Stephanie Meyer, a paranormal romance featuring vampires and werewolves, James decided to create her own fan fiction series, posted online as *Masters of the Universe*. It featured the two main characters of Meyer's work—Edward Cullen and Bella Swan—but put them into sexually explicit situations. Later James rewrote her material so that Cullen and Swan were original characters grounded in reality. (That is, she removed all mention of vampires and werewolves from her work.)

Other novelists who got their start writing fan fiction include Cassandra Clare and Naomi Novik. Clare wrote *Harry Potter* and *Lord of the Rings* fan fiction before turning her attention to wholly original works that include her *Mortal Instruments* fantasy series. Novik wrote *Star Trek* fan fiction before writing her *Temeraire* fantasy series.

The Line Between Fan Fiction and Plagiarism

The authors whose works inspire fan fiction have varying responses to other people's appropriation of their characters. J.K. Rowling, for example, endorses the creation of fan fiction based on her *Harry Potter* books, and television writer, director, and producer Joss Whedon has encouraged fans of his *Buffy the Vampire Slayer* TV series to read and write fan fiction based on the series. But George R.R. Martin, author of the *A Song of Ice and Fire* book series that begins with the novel *A Game of Thrones*, and Diana Gabaldon, author of the *Outlander* series, have spoken against fan fiction based on their work. Gabaldon says, "They're stealing an audience they're not entitled to."[11]

> "They're stealing an audience they're not entitled to."[11]
>
> —Diana Gabaldon, author of the *Outlander* series.

Indeed, some authors of fan fiction (whether in the form of books or movies) do get in trouble for stealing creative works, an act known as plagiarism. For example, in March 2016, the owners of the rights to the *Star Trek* franchise, CBS and Paramount Pictures, sued producer Alec Peters and his film company, Ax-

The Cost of Piracy

According to the Motion Picture Association of America, movie piracy costs the entertainment industry approximately $20.5 billion in lost revenue per year. Moreover, a study released in 2005 estimated that a 10 percent decrease in worldwide piracy of both movies and music would, over the course of four years, add 1.5 million jobs to the economy and result in an additional $64 billion in taxes and $400 billion in economic growth. Since that study is quite old, film expert Trevor Norkey says it is reasonable to believe that "those numbers are likely to be much higher today due to inflation and an increase in popularity of the film industry."

Revenue lost to piracy trickles down in a number of important ways. "The decrease in money from studios will often decrease the quality of other movies and even sequels, but more often it will decrease the quantity," explains Norkey. What he means is that studios become less likely to make franchise films (those with recurring characters) and sequels to films that have been heavily pirated, since they can expect to make much less money on them. Piracy also contributes to unemployment, because the fewer films are made, the fewer people are employed to work on them. This includes not just actors but hairdressers, electricians, caterers, drivers, and costume designers.

Trevor Norkey, "Film Piracy: A Threat to the Entire Movie Industry," Movie Pilot, April 26, 2015. http://moviepilot.com.

anar Productions, for creating a twenty-one-minute film, *Prelude to Axanar*, and developing a full-length feature film, *Axanar*, that features characters, settings, story elements, and many other aspects of the *Star Trek* series and movies, including the alien language Klingon developed specifically for *Star Trek* by linguist Marc Okrand.

Peters argues that he has the right to use so many proprietary aspects of *Star Trek* in his films because other *Star Trek* fans have done similar things without being sued. As he says, "[The rights holders] waived their rights because they let this [use of their material] go on for so long."[12] But legal experts say that this case is different because of the money involved. Typically, as long as the creators of fan books and films do not profit off their work and include enough original material to make it significantly different from the original, they will not be sued. However, Peters and his production company raised more than $650,000 for their feature film via crowdsourcing (whereby people put out an online call for donations to fund a project), and the similarities between their work and their source material are many. Matt Saccaro, who writes about media issues for *Salon*, argues that "ideas need to be stolen in

Klingons are depicted on the bridge of their battle cruiser in the film Star Trek the Motion Picture. *Producer Alec Peters got in legal trouble because his online fan films,* Prelude to Axanar *and* Axanar*, used characters, settings, and other story elements from the* Star Trek *television series and films.*

The Risk of Posting Unpublished Work

While some unpublished novelists have ended up getting an agent and/or a book contract as a result of sharing their work in online public forums, many experts say it is unwise to post unpublished fiction on the Internet. This is because, as editor and author Chuck Sambuchino reports, "You *cannot* copyright your ideas or concepts, so by putting stuff online, you are vulnerable." Sambuchino believes that the risk of having someone steal your ideas is far, far greater than the possibility of getting an agent. "Agents are busy people," he says. "They're not prowling around small writer blogs, of which there are thousands." Consequently, he says, "I do not advise posting fiction excerpts online just to see what happens. I have seen ideas get taken before, and I always advise writers on the safe side."

Chuck Sambuchino, "Be (Slightly) Afraid of Posting Your Work Online," *Writers Digest*, April 25, 2010. www.writersdigest.com.

order for plagiarism to exist."[13] Under this argument, some say, using the Klingon language in a *Star Trek* fan film should not warrant a lawsuit. Stealing story concepts and key plot points from the original television series, however, would definitely be illegal.

Some content producers have learned to live with fan fiction by seeing it as a promotion of their own work. Science-fiction writer Orson Scott Card is an example. Card, whose works include the novel *Ender's Game*, used to threaten to sue anyone who wrote fan fiction based on his writing—even going so far as to have his lawyer send out "cease and desist" letters warning of legal actions. Now, however, he encourages fans to create such work. "Every piece of fan fiction is an ad for my book," he explains. "What kind of idiot would I be to want that to disappear?"[14] Others think it is a mistake to sue people who are paying the ultimate homage to a piece of work and are likely the work's biggest advocates. Rebecca Tushnet is a copyright-law expert and a legal adviser to the Organization for Transformative Works, a nonprofit group that supports fan fiction. She puts the issue in the following way: "It's not good business to sue your customers."[15]

New Definitions?

Some people view Internet media as so different from traditional media that they think the long-standing rules related to drawing on others' work should not be applied to online creations. In fact, they argue that rules and laws need to change to keep pace with the new creative processes that online activities inspire. As Vicky Beeching, an expert in the ethics of online technology, says, "There's a lot to take on board about being in the digital world. It comes with a heck of a lot of issues, including how we delineate between our own ideas and other people's."[16]

An example of a type of creative work that some say is at odds with traditional rules is the mash-up, a recording or video made by combining content from a variety of different sources. Though technically each individual part of the mash-up should not be used without permission if the material is copyrighted, many people do not view those parts as being stolen. Instead they view them merely as the building blocks of a wholly unique product.

> "Authors can choose to sign with publishers, or they can reach readers on their own."[17]
>
> —Novelist J.A. Konrath.

Others note that the issue is as much about power as business. The Internet gives consumers more power than ever before—such as the power to affect public opinion through praise or ridicule, whether it concerns book or music sales or one's interpretation of a viral video. It also gives creative artists more power to shape their own careers. As novelist J.A. Konrath notes in regard to the publishing industry, "Authors can choose to sign with publishers, or they can reach readers on their own. And readers have more choice than ever, not simply what the gatekeepers chose. Publishers went from being the only game in town, to having to justify their existence."[17] Perhaps one day, he suggests, traditional forms of bringing creative works to market will no longer be important. In fact, they might even be obsolete.

CHAPTER TWO

Are Video Games Entertaining or Harmful?

Given the popularity that online video games currently enjoy, some might say playing them is the new American pastime. According to the Entertainment Software Association, which tracks video game use, in 2015 155 million people in the United States regularly played video games, and 42 percent of them played at least three hours a week. Among the gamers who played the most often, 39 percent played social games, and one in three played games that required them to purchase the game in order to play.

Online games are played via a personal computer, mobile device, or Internet-enabled game console, and there are many types of games to choose from. Some are fairly straightforward single-player games that involve completing word puzzles, fighting computer-controlled opponents in a boxing ring, or using a flight simulator to pilot a virtual aircraft. Others involve many players and complex strategies, such as coming together to conduct virtual military battles. Massively multiplayer online games (MMOGs) are among the most popular online games. Players often assume the role of characters (such as generals, knights, or soldiers) and interact with one another in real time within a fantasy or science-fiction setting.

Sharper Minds

Regardless of what a person plays, online gaming can be a pleasant way to pass spare moments, engage with others, and challenge the mind. In fact, studies have shown that playing video games has many mental benefits. For example, a study reported by the University of Iowa in 2013 found that people over the age of fifty who had played a matching game called *Road Tour* for at least ten hours showed, when checked a year later, a marked improvement in cognitive skills. Playing the game not only kept test subjects from losing mental agility as they aged, it actually made their minds sharper.

Other studies have shown mental improvements among younger players. For example, a 2013 study in Germany had people in their twenties play a racing game for thirty minutes a day over a two-month period, then examined their brains using a magnetic resonance imaging (MRI) machine. Researchers compared the results with brain scans of individuals who did not play the game. The scans of the gamers' brains showed positive changes in areas associated with spatial navigation, memory formation, strategizing, and fine motor skills that indicate their brains benefited from the gaming experience.

A group of friends enjoy playing a video game together. Many video games are played offline by individuals, but some of the most popular are massively multiplayer online games (MMOGs), in which many players compete with one another via an Internet connection.

Physical and Social Benefits

Other studies indicate that playing video games lowers stress and fear, distracts people from physical pain, and improves certain aspects of eyesight. For example, a joint study by researchers at the University of Rochester in New York and the Goldschleger Eye Research Institute in Israel found that playing a first-person shooter game could increase contrast sensitivity, which enables people to detect small increments in shades of gray on a uniform background and to discern small changes in degrees of brightness. The researchers believe this is due to the exercise a player's eyes get as the player locates, aims, and shoots at a target.

Playing video games offers some social benefits, too. In 2013 psychology experts at Racboud University in the Netherlands reviewed research related to gaming and concluded that playing multiplayer games helps children develop cooperative skills. Moreover, games that feature social communities teach children how to lead a group, how to determine whom to trust or reject, and how to make quick decisions. The researchers also concluded that playing video games can help children learn to cope with failure, thereby making them more emotionally resilient.

Encouraging Socially Unacceptable Behavior

But some of what people learn from video games is not so positive. For example, some games, like those in the *Grand Theft Auto* series, have players act out criminal behavior; other games might not require players to commit virtual crimes but still show these crimes being committed without any negative consequences for the criminal. Experts worry that both types of games can make players think that such behavior is acceptable in the real world.

Indeed, detective Jamie Saunders of the National Crime Agency in the United Kingdom has come across many cases in which a cybercriminal—a person who commits serious crimes using a computer—began stealing things as a young person in the context of playing an online game. "There are some sorts of criminality that youngsters don't think of as serious," says Saunders. "Stealing gold off each other in online games, cheating if you like. It would be hard to imagine a knock on the door from a policeman because you've stolen a sword off your friend in World of Warcraft."[18] With age, this attitude could lead gamers who once stole online treasure to see nothing wrong with going after bigger hauls, such as personal data or credit card account numbers.

Studies also suggest that video games that feature racist and sexist behavior can make that behavior seem acceptable in the real world. *Grand Theft Auto V*, for example, features extreme violence and depicts women as sex objects (generally as strippers, prostitutes, or set decorations). "There are three lead characters that players can control in the game: all male," reports game critic Tom Hoggins. "The women characters are often leered at or cast as

Copies of Grand Theft Auto IV, *a game in which players participate in virtual crimes, are prominently displayed for sale. Some experts say that when players participate in such games, the lack of actual consequences may lead participants to believe that criminal behavior is acceptable in the real world.*

nags. One of the player character's daughters has 'skank' tattooed across her back, one mission has you chaperoning a paparazzo as he tries to photograph an aging actress's [genital area]."[19]

Hoggins is one of many men who find such depictions of women distasteful. "How wretched I felt as the game often coerced me into actions that degraded women,"[20] he recalls. Other men, however, are either unbothered by such sexism or quickly grow accustomed to it. Either way, experts believe this leads at least some men to make sexist remarks to women, and especially female players. Canadian media expert Matthew Johnson reports: "One study found that playing *Halo 3* with a female voice and a female-identifying name led to three times more negative comments than playing with a male voice and a male-identifying name or no voice and a gender-neutral name."[21] Game designer Manveer Heir worries that negative depictions of women and minorities "affect the way people think and treat others in the real world, and perpetuate the social injustices that occur in these different groups."[22]

> "How wretched I felt as the game often coerced me into actions that degraded women"[20]
>
> —Tom Hoggins, video game critic.

Others counter that the majority of gamers know that what is acceptable in a game world is not necessarily acceptable in the real world. In the case of *Grand Theft Auto V*, for example, gamer and entertainment/technology writer Erik Kain says that such games are intended to be enjoyed by adults, most of whom have the ability to see the game as fantasy. "We can drive through stop lights, mow over civilians, crash and die and start over, get in ridiculous gunfights and still walk away on two feet. Or even just go shopping, or play golf, or hunt," he says. "We are given a vast canvas of possibilities, and the freedom to pretend to break bad in a cartoonish, outlandish, alternative reality. Most people can see this for what it is: escapism."[23]

Increased Aggression

Others note that when a gamer engages in bad behavior both online and offline, it is difficult, if not impossible, to say that the online behavior caused the offline behavior. Indeed, this issue has not been settled despite much study into whether there is a cause-and-effect relationship between playing violent video games and engaging in violent behavior. A great deal of such research has shown that playing violent video games does increase aggression, however, and that this effect can become more pronounced over time. For example, a 2013 study by researchers at Ohio State University found that people who played a violent video game for three consecutive days showed an increase each day in aggressive behavior and hostility.

In addition, many studies have shown that playing violent video games makes players less compassionate, empathetic, and helpful to others. A 2014 study by researchers at the University of Illinois Urbana-Champaign also found that a player's selection of game character is connected to the player's behavior in the real world. Specifically, someone who chooses to be a hero in a game tends to treat real people well, while those who choose to play as a villain tend to treat real people in negative ways.

> "More than any other media, [first-person shooter] video games encourage active participation in violence."[24]
>
> —Psychology professor Bruce Bartholow of the University of Missouri.

Some experts also believe that playing online games might increase the likelihood of committing violent crimes, as suggested by a study reported in 2013 by researchers with Iowa State University. They looked at the amount of violent game playing by 227 juvenile offenders in Pennsylvania who had committed several serious acts of violence, including gang fighting and attacking their parents, within the prior year. They found a strong association between playing violent video games and juvenile delinquency. This was true even after they accounted for many other factors, such as exposure to violence in the home, time spent watching TV, and the age the offenders first ended up in juvenile court.

First-Person Shooter Games

Research has also supported the contention that first-person shooter games encourage real-world violence. In fact, some ex-

Arresting Gamers

In 2014 online video game players in Japan were put on notice that cheating can have serious consequences. Police arrested three teens for using cheat tools and distributing them to other players, and the teens were charged with obstruction of business. The following year, three more teens were arrested for cheating in a game because their actions had enabled them to obtain weapons and other items for free instead of paying for them.

Whether the real justice world should be brought into the virtual world of video games is of great debate. Nexon, the gaming company that initiated the complaints, argues that cheaters negatively impact players' experiences and potentially hurt sales. Cheating, in their mind, is akin to stealing. However, Timothy Geigner, who writes for TechDirt.com on gaming-related legal issues, believes that arrests and fines are far too great a punishment for cheating in a video game, especially since gamers can have a hard time distinguishing between cheating and simply gaining an advantage in the game. "It's reasonable to argue that if the game maker *allows* something to happen in the game, then it's on that game maker to set things up to block actions it doesn't like," he says. "Opening it up to the criminal justice system seems like a recipe for disaster."

Timothy Geigner, "The Future Is Now: Cheating in Online Games Leads to Arrests in Japan," TechDirt, June 27, 2014. www.techdirt.com.

perts believe that first-person shooter games can train people to kill. According to Bruce Bartholow, an associate professor of psychology at the University of Missouri, "More than any other media, these video games encourage active participation in violence."[24]

As evidence, Bartholow and others point to cases in which such games appear to have influenced a killer. For example, Anders Behring Breivik of Oslo, Norway, in July 2011 launched an assault on a summer camp for teens that killed sixty-nine people and wounded sixty-six. Breivik later reported that his experiences playing the first-person shooter game *Call of Duty: Modern Warfare* affected how he carried out his massacre. For example, he equipped his gun with a holographic sight similar to the one he used in the game because of how well it worked. Had he not done this, he said, he might not have been able to kill so many people. At his trial, Breivik testified that playing *Call of Duty* was akin to using a training simulator because it "consists of many hundreds of different tasks and some of these tasks can be compared with an attack, for real. That's why it's used by many armies throughout the world."[25]

The Will to Kill?

Indeed, many armies do incorporate video game play into their training programs, as do some law enforcement agencies. This practice is based on long-standing research showing that first-person shooter games can improve a shooter's accuracy. For example, a 2012 Ohio State University study found that just twenty minutes of playing a first-person shooter game made participants more accurate when firing at a mannequin.

However, many others disagree. Journalist Paul Tassi, who has written extensively on issues pertaining to video games, for example, does not believe that this degree of accuracy carries over to situations involving real people, since firing at a person is different from firing at a target shaped like a person. After all, virtual victims do not spill actual blood, nor do their deaths bring criminal charges. Consequently, Tassi insists that "being good at Call of Duty makes you about as competent a soldier as playing Dr. Mario makes you a cardiovascular surgeon."[26]

But Dave Grossman, a retired lieutenant colonel in the US Army, argues that video games can train people to become effective killers. As evidence he points to the case of fourteen-year-old

> "Being good at Call of Duty makes you about as competent a soldier as playing Dr. Mario makes you a cardiovascular surgeon."[26]
>
> —Journalist Paul Tassi.

Michael Carneal of Paducah, Kentucky, an avid player of the first-person shooter game *Doom*. Despite no prior shooting experience, Carneal shot at eight schoolmates and hit all of them, five in the head and three in the upper torso. "Nowhere in the annals of military or law enforcement history can we find an equivalent 'achievement,'"[27] Grossman reports.

The Ohio State study suggests that experience with video games might also influence the type of shots people take. Specifically, those twenty minutes of playing a first-person shooter

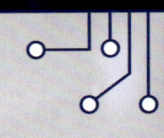

Playing Video Games May Help Improve Dyslexia

While there are some concerns over children playing video games, a 2013 study from the University of Padua in Italy suggests that there may be some benefits to children between ages seven and thirteen who have dyslexia, a learning disability that affects a person's ability to read and spell words. Specifically, action video games may help improve such children's reading skills.

In the study, dyslexic children's abilities were tested both before and after twelve hours of game play, and the results were striking. Not only did the children read faster, but they also showed improvement in both text reading and the phonetic decoding of words (whereby words are sounded out). In fact, their improvement exceeded what one would expect to see after a year of reading development sessions.

game made individuals more likely to take a "kill shot"—that is, to fire at the head rather than the torso. Indeed, given where Carneal's bullets struck, he was apparently aiming for his victims' heads, just as he would have done while playing *Doom*. Consequently one of the authors of the Ohio State study, psychologist Brad Bushman, says it is clear that "for good and bad, video game players are learning lessons that can be applied in the real world."[28]

A Cocktail of Causes

However, other real-world factors further confuse the relationship between video games and violence. This includes one's living conditions. For example, suppose someone who commits a mass shooting not only plays first-person shooter games but also comes from a violent household. How can it be determined whether it was the game or the household, or both, that influenced his or her actions? Indeed, it is also possible that something else entirely was to blame.

In 2015 the American Psychological Association established a task force to study this issue further. The task force's chair, Mark Appelbaum, is one of many who argue that violence is a complicated issue that is likely driven by more than one factor. "What researchers need to do now is conduct studies that look at the effects of video game play in people at risk for aggression or violence due to a combination of risk factors," says Appelbaum. "For example, how do depression or delinquency interact with violent video game use?"[29]

Doug Gentile, a research psychologist and associate professor at Iowa State University, agrees. Considering all of the factors that might be involved in the making of a mass shooter, he says,

> The truth of the matter is that there is never one cause. There is a cocktail of multiple causes coming together. And so no matter what single thing we focus on, whether it be violent video games, abuse as a child, doing drugs, being in a gang—not one of them is sufficient to cause aggression. But when you start putting them together, aggression becomes pretty predictable.[30]

Mental Illness

The relationship between mental illness and violent video games is another ongoing topic of investigation. This issue surfaced yet again after the 2012 mass shooting of twenty children and six adults at Sandy Hook Elementary School in Newtown, Connecticut. After the attack the media made much of the fact that Adam Lanza (the twenty-year-old perpetrator) played *Call of Duty*, among other games. The implication was that Lanza's enjoyment of violent video games was the key to understanding why he went on a shooting rampage.

However, experts believe Lanza's mental state (dating back to his teen years) was the more significant factor. By the time Lanza had reached adulthood, he was exhibiting disturbing behavior that included refusing to come out of his room, covering his windows with black garbage bags, and going for days without eating. He also had a preoccupation with mass murder and a fascination with guns. On the morning of the Sandy Hook shooting he killed his mother in her bedroom before heading to the school. He killed himself shortly after police arrived.

Given Lanza's personal history, experts acknowledge there is no way to know how big a role video games played in the shooting. "It is impossible to know whether playing violent video games causes violent criminal behavior such as the Newtown shootings, because in our laboratory experiments we can't give people guns to see if they shoot each other with them,"[31] admits Bushman. Moreover, when a mass shooter is male and in his teens or early twenties—as Lanza and many other mass shooters have been—it would be unusual if he did *not* play violent video games, since according to a 2015 Pew research study 84 percent of teenage boys play such games (and 72 percent of teens as a whole play video games). In other words, since nearly all young men play at least one violent video game, it is highly likely that those young men who commit mass shootings—of which there are relatively few—will also have played a violent video game.

Small Numbers

Indeed, it is important to stress that although large numbers of people play violent online games, only a tiny fraction of them become killers. This fact is enough to cast doubt on the extent to which video games are responsible for violence. As Kain says: "If it were true, millions of your neighbors, kids, and co-workers would be violent killers. So far as I can tell, this is not the case."[32] Because so few gamers appear to succumb to the negative effects of playing violent video games, experts say that more research is needed into what types of people might be the most susceptible to these effects.

CHAPTER THREE

Concerns About Online Pornography

Pornography is material that is sexually explicit and intended to stimulate erotic feelings. Experts report that there are at least 4 million pornographic websites online and that at least one-fourth of daily search engine requests are related to pornography. Moreover, surveys indicate that more than 40 percent of Internet users have viewed some type of pornography online. Given the interest in sexually explicit material, pornography has become big business. In fact, according to business experts, in 2015 the pornography industry took in more than $97 billion globally. (By comparison, the video game industry took in approximately $91.5 billion globally that year; the movie production and distribution industry, $90 billion; and the music production and distribution industry, $15 billion.)

Technological Advances

Pornography, then, can be considered a major entertainment industry. But it is also responsible for significant business and technological advances that have positively impacted other industries. For example, the pornography industry pioneered various aspects of e-commerce, including online credit card transactions. As Frederick Lane, author of *Obscene Profits: The Entrepreneurs of Pornography in the Cyber Age*, reports, the industry "convincingly demonstrated that consumers are willing to shop online and are willing to use credit cards to make purchases."

Lane adds that the industry was also at the forefront of such practices as establishing monthly site fees, using free material as a lure to attract more visitors to a website, and upselling, whereby people who have subscribed to a site are encouraged to buy related services. Consequently, he says, "In myriad ways, large and small, the porn industry has blazed a commercial path that other industries are hastening to follow."[33]

The pornography industry has also been responsible for technological advances related to film production and distribution. For example, it invested in the development of software that could add subtitles and closed captioning to films. It was also instrumental in the spread of webcams and the popularization of video chats, and pioneered video streaming. In fact, computer technology expert Paul Rudo reports that the first workable Internet-based streaming system was developed by a Dutch pornography company in 1994. "Without streaming pornography, today's webcasts—from presidential addresses to viral kitten videos—would still be the stuff of science fiction,"[34] says Rudo.

Not for Minors

Of course, the pornography industry also entertains many people. While some say it enhances their personal relationships, experts point out that under certain circumstances and/or for certain people, online pornography can damage both individuals and relationships. This is particularly true when young people are exposed to online pornography, either as viewers or as participants in its creation.

In the United States, it is legal for adults to view online pornography, provided it is not obscene and does not depict children. According to the US Supreme Court, pornography can be considered obscene if it depicts "patently offensive hard core sexual conduct."[35] However, since deciding what might fall into this category involves a subjective judgment, and because the Internet is hard to police, authorities typically concern themselves only with enforcing laws that prohibit child pornography. This is not only because it is easier to recognize what constitutes child pornography

but also because the making of such pornography typically does great harm to the children involved.

Given this, authorities commit a great many resources to finding and arresting the people who traffic in child pornography. For example, law enforcement agencies might create fake websites that will trick pedophiles—people who sexually prey on children—into thinking they are about to obtain child pornography. Federal agents might also work with companies that control Internet web pages and/or offer e-mail accounts in order to gain access to customer account details.

Webcam Tricks

One of the ways that pornography can get online is via webcams, cameras within a computer that can transmit images via the Internet. These images can be viewed in real time, and can be saved for later viewing as well. Consequently pornographers often use webcams as a way to acquire sexually explicit images of teens—but without telling their victims who they really are or what the webcam images will actually be used for. This was the case in Rotterdam, Netherlands, where a thirty-four-year-old man tricked dozens of underage girls, including ones with mental disabilities, into engaging in sexual acts in front of webcams, typically on their bedroom computers. He told many of them that he was a music industry representative, suggesting that he could put them in contact with pop celebrities. Instead he victimized them.

Another way agents can track down pedophiles is by first finding the children whose images have been shared online, then investigating anyone in their lives to see who might have created the images. This approach is necessary when pornographers share images via a darknet, a network within the Internet that allows for complete anonymity. Anonymity networks are often used for illegal file sharing because they prevent activities from being monitored and traced.

Such was the situation with fourteen pornographers who were arrested in 2014 by the US Department of Homeland Security. These criminals had conspired to acquire nude and seminude images of teens and share them with sexual predators worldwide via a darknet commonly known as TOR (because it uses software associated with a type of router, The Onion Router, to direct Internet traffic through the anonymity network). By studying not only the faces but background details in these photos, federal officials managed to find 251 of the victims, who were located in thirty-seven US states and five foreign countries.

Many of the teens—most of whom were males between the ages of thirteen and fifteen—did not even realize they had been victimized. This is because the pornographers interacted with their victims only online while pretending to be teenagers themselves. Through these conversations, victims were coaxed into sending suggestive photos of themselves to the pornographer and/or striking suggestive poses during webchats that many of the teens did not know were being recorded. Consequently, Lynn Davis, head of the Dallas Children's Advocacy Center in Texas where nineteen of the victims were located, says, "Some of these kids will still not consider themselves victims until one day they wake up and realize, 'I sent some pictures out there.' And once those pictures are on the Internet you can never get them back."[36]

Inadvertent Glimpses

Another way that children can be victimized by online pornography is by accidentally coming across such images while searching the Internet. Experts do not know just how harmful this experience can be, because no one conducting studies on the effects of pornography on children is willing to expose children to such images in order to measure their responses. However, based on studies of the behavior of teens who viewed pornography as young children, some experts believe it makes young people more accepting of casual sex, more likely to become sexually active at a young age, and/or more likely to become promiscuous. (Other experts believe that there is not enough evidence to support these findings, however.)

Most experts agree that viewing pornography at a young age is not ideal, least of all because of the messages that pornography sends about sex. In fact, teens themselves worry about this issue. UK psychologist Miranda Horvath, who has researched the impact of pornography on children in England, reports that when a group of teens between the ages of sixteen and eighteen was asked to debate whether pornography negatively impacted young people, those in the "yes" camp felt it could harm their body image and pressure them to behave in certain ways. She reports, "They talked about how if you see things in pornography, you might think it's something you should be doing and go and do it."[37]

Another researcher, psychologist Rory Reid of the University of California, Los Angeles (UCLA), believes pornography can influence teens' attitudes towards sex, and not for the better. As Reid puts it, "I have a son, and I don't want him getting his information about human sexuality from Internet porn because the vast majority of such material contains fraudulent messages about sex—that all women have insatiable sexual appetites, for example."[38]

Because children can get false ideas about sex from pornography, Horvath says that they need to be educated about sex before being allowed unsupervised access to the Internet. "Children should be taught about relationships and sex at a young age," she says. "If we start teaching kids about equality and respect when they are 5 or 6 years old, by the time they encounter porn in their teens, they will be able to pick out and see the lack of respect and emotion that porn gives us. They'll be better equipped to deal with what they are being presented with."[39]

Sexting

Education is also an issue when it comes to teens who voluntarily pose for pornographic pictures, or take ones of themselves. Many experts say that young people need to be made aware of the risks involved with this practice, which often results in pictures being texted, or sexted, to others and posted online. Various surveys indicate that as many as 50 percent of those under the age of eighteen have sexted, with at least 20 percent sending sexually explicit photos or videos.

The biggest risk related to teen sexting concerns its legality. Under federal and many state laws, the possession or transmission of a sexually explicit image of a minor is a crime because it is considered a form of child pornography. This is true even if the person who has the image received it without asking for it. It is also true even if the subject of the photo is the person who took it. Consequently a teenager who takes a sexually explicit selfie and sexts it to someone else can be charged with three felony crimes: promoting, distributing, and possessing child pornography. This means that most teen sexting activities are crimes. But as psychologist James Wellborn reports, students "don't understand the profound legal implications. They think they're just trading pictures."[40]

Instead, sexting teens could end up with lengthy prison sentences. In the state of Illinois, for example, anyone who videotapes or photographs a nude or seminude person whom he or she should know is under the age of eighteen can be charged with a Class 1 felony that comes with a mandatory fine of $2,000 to $100,000 and at least four years of prison. No exception is

The Children's Internet Protection Act

Enacted in 2000, the Children's Internet Protection Act (CIPA) requires that public schools as well as some libraries use Internet filtering or blocking software to prevent minors from accessing any online material, including pornography, that would be considered harmful to them. But while the intent of this law is good, critics say it is often misused. Rainey Reitman, one of the directors of the Electronic Frontier Foundation, explains that even though they are not required to, libraries end up blocking social networking sites, political sites, sites that advocate for gay/lesbian issues, sites about art (which may feature nudity), or sites that explore controversial issues such as gun control or abortion. As a result, "libraries across the country are routinely overblocking content, censoring far more than is necessary under the law," says Reitman. "This means library patrons are cut off from whole swaths of the World Wide Web, hampering their access to knowledge."

Rainey Reitman, "The Cost of Censorship in Libraries: 10 Years Under the Children's Internet Protection Act," Electronic Frontier Foundation, September 4, 2013. www.eff.org.

made for offenders whose videos and photos have been of themselves. This is why four high school students in Joliet, Illinois, all between the ages of fourteen and sixteen, were arrested on felony charges after they posted on Twitter a video of themselves engaging in consensual sex acts. Their post came to the attention of authorities after the mother of one of the girls in the video found out about it and reported it to police.

Joliet police chief Brian Benton later defended the children's arrest by saying, "The child pornography offense that was charged is in place for a reason, because we don't want to accept that type of behavior as a society. It's making a strong statement, and I think it's important to do so, to send a message to others that kids shouldn't be involved in this type of behavior."[41]

Harassment

But criminal charges are not the only reason not to send sexually provocative images of oneself online. Embarrassment and harassment are others. This is particularly true when teens are involved, because those who have shared nude photos of themselves often become objects of ridicule at school and beyond.

This happened to Allyson Pereira, who is now an antibullying advocate. When she was a sophomore at a New Jersey high school her boyfriend broke up with her, then said they could get back together if she sexted him a nude photo of herself. When she did, he shared it online. Immediately Pereira was harassed by classmates, both at school and online.

Then things calmed down at school—only to resurface at work two years later. She reports, "I was working as a waitress when my boss told me he had heard about the picture. He told me he was going to have it sent to him, rate it, and he'd let me know what he thought." The picture haunted her yet again when she "volunteered for a local school committee and was eating lunch when a group of girls took out their phones and showed the picture to security guards. I hid in a corner while they all pointed and laughed."[42] Pereira says these experiences and others significantly altered her life: "I didn't go away to college because I feared my dorm mates would find out about it and hate me."[43]

Experts in teen psychology, such as Raychelle Cassada Lohmann, say that the repercussions of having one's nude or seminude images shared with others without permission can make life almost unbearable for teens "Oftentimes they don't reach out for help because of embarrassment and disappointment, fear of making it worse, or fear of getting into trouble," she says. Many teens "may feel like they're caught in a trap with no way out."[44]

Search Results

Teens whose sexually suggestive or explicit images appear online can also be blocked from certain experiences or even job offers. Because individuals who have willingly posed for such images are often looked down upon, some employers may not hire someone

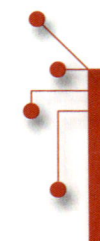

who has such photos online. Furthermore, surveys have shown that those in a position to offer jobs or admission to college are increasingly likely to search the Internet for information on applicants.

The increasing importance of one's digital reputation means that just one pornographic photo or video of an individual online can do a lifetime of damage. Moreover, because of the vast reach of the Internet, a person's reputation can be global. As the community service minister of Australia's state government of New South Wales, Linda Burney, says: "It is frightening to think that once these images are online or on a phone, anyone anywhere in the world can access them. It is then impossible to retrieve and delete them. They are there forever and can damage future career prospects or relationships."[45]

Less Committed

Indeed, relationships can suffer when one member of a couple comes across an online pornographic photo or video of the other without prior knowledge of its existence. Relationships can also suffer when one partner of a couple is viewing pornography against the other's wishes, and not just because of the arguments that result. Studies have shown that individuals who watch online pornography are less committed to their partners. In reporting on such studies, psychologist Syras Derksen says: "In one experiment some randomly chosen men were shown pornography and, afterwards, these men were more likely to see other women as romantic alternatives."[46] This confirms what many psychologists believe: that someone watching pornography is imagining being with another partner—and perhaps fantasizing about being free to pursue someone else in real life.

Derksen reports that in one experiment, men who regularly viewed porn were required to stop viewing it for three weeks,

A man uses a tablet to surf the Internet while lying in bed. Studies have shown that people who view pornographic photos or videos become less committed to their partners.

and at the end of this period all said they felt more committed to their relationship. Similarly, a 2012 study from researchers at the University of Florida found that among people between the ages of seventeen and twenty-six, porn viewing lowered commitment levels for both men and women. Other studies have shown that men who view porn are less likely to communicate with a partner in a way that, to an objective observer, shows that the two are committed to one another. In addition, porn viewers are more likely to flirt during online chats with strangers.

Damaged Families

In addition to weakening commitment, pornography can tear families apart, particularly when the user is addicted to the activity. An obsession with pornography can result in a host of other problems as well, including lost jobs, poor personal habits, and ill health. Moreover, some experts say it is easier to develop an addiction to pornography than to drugs or alcohol because it is

easier and quicker to access pornography than it is to acquire drugs or alcohol.

Watching too much online pornography can also cause psychological problems. As family physician Marysia Weber explains, "Internet pornography leaves people wanting more and more, but they may not necessarily like what they see, which contributes to symptoms of anxiety and depression. Over time, your senses dull and it's harder to find pleasure in the images, or even in everyday life."[47] When viewed in moderation, however, online pornography can be a healthy addition to the sexual life of many adults—although experts stress that as with other Internet activities, online pornography should not be viewed as a substitute for meaningful real-world relationships and should never be consumed by or feature children.

CHAPTER FOUR

When Online Entertainment Becomes Addictive

While online entertainment enhances many lives, some individuals find themselves so obsessed with it that they cannot function. Experts generally say that such people can be considered to be addicted to the Internet. According to the Center for Internet Addiction—a treatment center for Internet addicts founded by psychologist and Internet addiction expert Kimberly Young—online addiction is defined as "any online-related, compulsive behavior which interferes with normal living and causes severe stress on family, friends, loved ones, and one's work environment."[48]

People who find it difficult or impossible to limit the time they spend online can be drawn to a variety of activities. Some are addicted to texting, others to surfing the web, and still others to using social media sites. Many Internet addicts tend to have other addictions as well.

Is Online Gaming a Disorder?

Among those who cannot control their online entertainment activities are those who are addicted to online video games. In fact, excessive Internet gaming is such a problem that the most recent edition of the American Psychiatric Association's (APA) *Diagnostic and Statistical Manual of Mental Disorders* (DSM-5)—which establishes standard criteria for classifying mental disorders—states that the condition warrants more clinical research, and that it might consider identifying Internet gaming addiction as a disorder in a future edition of the manual. In explaining why online gaming deserves this consideration, the APA says:

> The "gamers" play compulsively, to the exclusion of other interests, and their persistent and recurrent online activity results in clinically significant impairment or distress. People with this condition endanger their academic or job functioning because of the amount of time they spend playing. They experience symptoms of withdrawal when pulled away from gaming.[49]

Many addiction experts already believe that compulsive gaming is a disorder. In fact, the Center for Internet Addiction defines Internet gaming disorder as "an addiction to online video games, role-playing games, or any interactive gaming environment available through the Internet." The center says that games with extensive chat features are more likely to trigger this disorder because such features "give such games a social aspect missing from offline activities, and the collaborative/competitive nature of working with or against other players can make it hard to take a break."[50]

Being Hooked

An example of how a person can be adversely impacted by such games is twenty-four-year-old Daniel, who lives in the United Kingdom. He told Tom Meltzer, a reporter with the *Guardian*, that he had been playing video games obsessively since the age of seven. However, his addiction to the activity did not become a serious problem until his teenage years. "I was playing 15 hours a day at the peak," says Daniel. "The worst year I can remember was when I was playing EverQuest. I was 16, and I was getting up at two in the morning and going downstairs on to my mum's

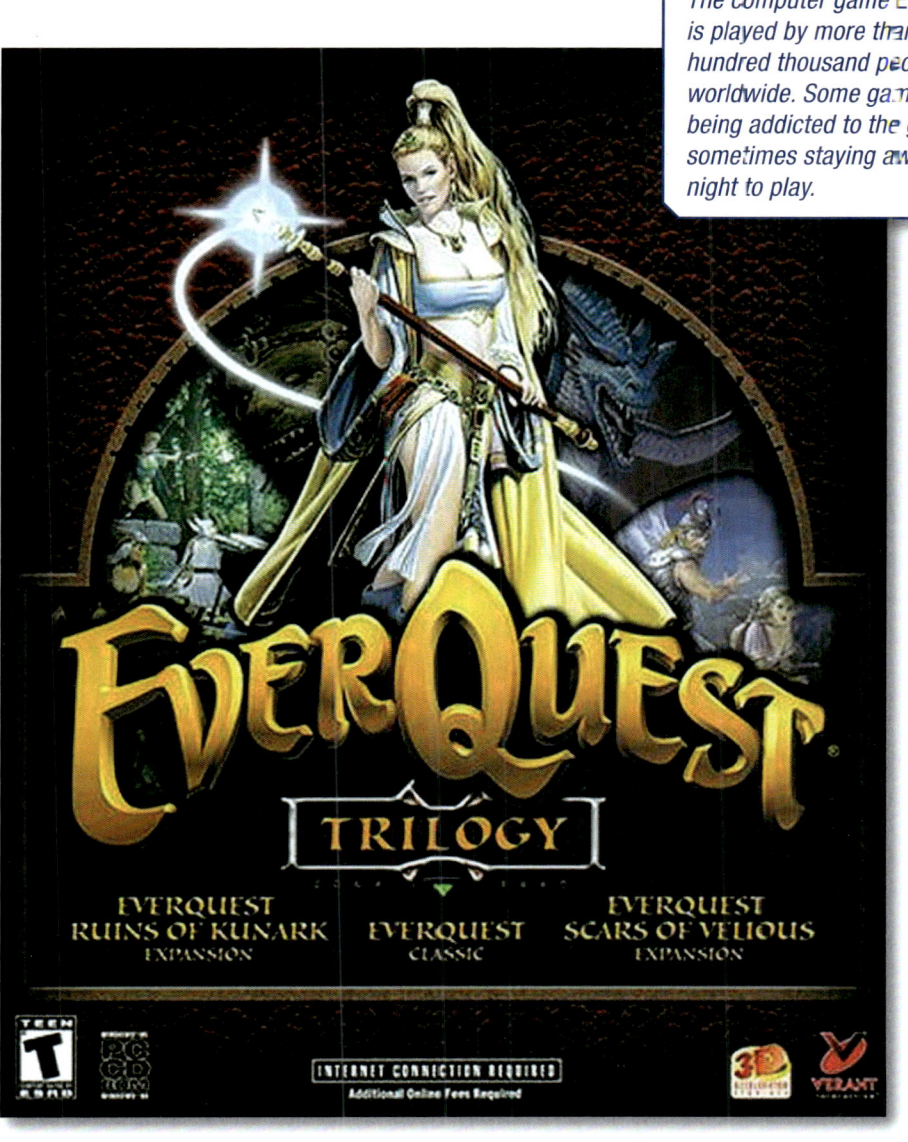

laptop to play. I was up until eight, and then I'd get back into bed saying I was ill."[51]

Daniel says playing video games made him feel better about himself, since he was an expert at it. "Experience had made me good at [video games], and being good made them reliable sources of self-esteem," he says. "Games were the one place as a weedy, nervous teenager that I could, as I would have said then, kick ass."[52]

Teen Gamblers

Most countries have laws intended to prevent minors from gambling, but the anonymity of the Internet makes enforcing them difficult. Whereas gambling casinos in the real world must check the IDs of individuals who look underage, there is no legitimate system for doing this online. Consequently, it can be easy for teens to use a credit card to register at online casinos or card rooms.

In fact, according to the National Institutes of Health, up to 25 percent of adolescents with serious gambling problems report that they use online gambling sites. As a result, the number of teen gambling addicts is becoming a significant problem in the United States and worldwide. According to the International Centre for Youth Gambling Problems and High-Risk Behaviors at Canada's McGill University, roughly 4 percent to 5 percent of young people between the ages of twelve and seventeen exhibit at least one symptom of a gambling problem. Another 10 percent to 14 percent have lost so much control over their gambling that they can be considered at risk of developing an addiction. In addition, between 60 percent and 80 percent of high school students say they have gambled for money during the past year, 6 percent to 8 percent say their gambling feels out of control, and 4 percent to 6 percent can be considered addicted to gambling.

Meltzer admits that for similar reasons, he too was a gaming addict. "Daniel's story is not so different from my own," he says. "We were both miserable as teens, and we both played truant in the fantasy world of games."[53] Meltzer confesses that he missed an average of one day of school a week throughout the academic year. Daniel's attendance was even worse. In his first year of secondary school, before he became a gaming addict, he had a perfect attendance record. By his last year of secondary school his 100 percent record had fallen to 45 percent.

In the most extreme cases of game addiction, players can miss more than just school or work. They can skip meals and important aspects of personal hygiene, such as brushing their teeth and showering. Some also become severely sleep deprived.

MMOGs and MMORPGs

It is no coincidence that *EverQuest* brought out Daniel's most addictive behavior. This is because it is a massively multiplayer online role-playing game (MMORPG), which means that players interact with thousands of other players as a character in the game world. Psychologists and others who treat gaming addictions largely agree that highly social games are most likely to trigger an addiction, and that MMOGs are the most addictive of all video games. As Daniel notes, "You can't play for a little bit with these games. You have to play for a lot or not at all."[54]

According to the Guinness Book of World Records, the most popular MMORPG as of November 2015 was *World of Warcraft*, or *WoW*. Many of its more than 5 million subscribers love the game, but have also complained about the way it interferes with daily life. This includes poet and writing teacher Ryan van Cleave, who wrote the first memoir on video game addiction, *Unplugged: My Journey into the Dark World of Video Game Addiction*, in 2010.

While in the midst of his addiction, van Cleave was attempting to work as a university English professor. But because he was devoting roughly sixty hours a week to *WoW* and skipping sleep in the process, he soon lost his job. He developed health problems and became emotionally unstable. He also spent a lot of money supporting his addiction, on both the subscription fees required to play the game and on in-game purchases to improve weaponry and other playing features. This further added to stress, not only on him but on his family. His wife threatened to leave him, and van Cleave felt that his children had begun to hate him.

> **"You can't play for a little bit with these games. You have to play for a lot or not at all."[54]**
>
> —Daniel, a self-professed online video game addict.

Others noted that van Cleave was not the same person he used to be. He became noticeably moody and difficult. His best friend from high school and *WoW* gaming buddy, Rob Opitz, noted that when things in the real world interrupted their gameplay, van Cleave "would get very loud very quickly about those things. During that time it's kind of like everything was completely over the top. It wasn't that he was a little mad, he was in a full-blown rage."[55]

Gaming Addiction Treatment

Van Cleave eventually became so disgusted with his behavior that he deleted *WoW* from his computer and fought the urge to return to playing the game. This approach enabled him to overcome his gaming addiction. But others need help kicking their habit. Some seek out individual counseling. Others turn to group programs and/or facilities that specialize in treating Internet addiction.

One example of such a facility is the Center for Internet and Technology Addiction in West Hartford, Connecticut. It offers two- and five-day intensive treatment programs on an outpatient basis, which means that patients are free to come and go in between sessions. Another facility is reSTART, a Seattle-area Internet addiction treatment center that requires patients to live at the center for a period of weeks or months, completely cut off from all access to technology. Inpatient treatment programs last seven to ten weeks, during which patients participate in therapy sessions and develop skills that help them cope with technological temptation once they leave the center.

Hilarie Cash, one of reSTART's founders, says of the center's patients, "Most of the people that come are young adult males around the ages of 18 to 30 who spend a lot of time on the Internet. Their health is poor, their social relationships have turned to crap, they have no social confidence or real-world friends. They don't date. They don't work."[56]

Online Gambling

A different kind of gaming some people become addicted to is online gambling. In fact, experts in gambling addiction say that gambling in an online casino is more likely to trigger an addiction than gambling in a real-life casino. There are several reasons why. Among them is the fact that online gambling can be done both conveniently and privately, away from the prying eyes of friends, family, or coworkers. Another is that online casinos often allow gamblers to play for free for a certain amount of time, which gets them accustomed not only to the game but to thinking that their losses aren't really losses. Often these free-to-play games provide better odds of winning, thereby lulling players into thinking that they have a good chance of winning once they play for money.

In actuality, though, it is easy to lose money at online gambling, something sixty-two-year-old Sheila Muir of the United Kingdom learned firsthand. At first the games she played on the Kitty Bingo

A recovering Internet addict cooks his dinner with the help of one of the cofounders of the reSTART Internet Addiction Recovery Program. reSTART is a residential treatment center where patients spend weeks or even months learning how to cope with their technology addiction.

website, which offers roulette as well as bingo, were pleasant, easy, and fun. But soon she found herself hooked on the site and losing as much as a thousand British pounds (slightly more than $1,400 USD) a day. "I won at first and when I started to lose I played again to try to make the money back," she says. "Because it was online, it was like Monopoly money. I didn't notice it had gone."[57] Before she knew it, she had lost 20,000 pounds in cash (roughly $28,500) and reached her 6,000-pound (just over $8,500) credit card limit.

Liz Karter, a therapist who specializes in treating gambling addictions, says women like Muir (who had recently lost her job) are often dealing with personal problems when they succumb to Internet addiction. "Many of the women I speak to don't gamble online for the thrill of winning; it's about finding a way of escaping their problems for a few hours," says Karter. "While some people might turn to alcohol or drugs, these women have such busy lives that's not possible. With gambling, you can escape your problems, but still get up to go to work in the morning or look after the baby."[58]

Forty-year-old Caroline Owen nearly lost her home because money earmarked to pay her mortgage went toward funding her online gambling addiction. Now, Owen thinks that such addictions are primarily driven by a desire to escape. "For me, it was never about the thrill of winning," she says. "The websites would allow me to switch off completely and not to think about any of my problems. I would describe myself as being in a kind of zombie state."[59]

> "Many of the women I speak to don't gamble online for the thrill of winning; it's about finding a way of escaping their problems for a few hours."[58]
>
> —Liz Karter, a therapist who specializes in treating gambling addictions.

Binge-Watching Addictions

A desire to escape one's problems can also drive another online activity that can become compulsive: binge-watching, or viewing multiple episodes of a television series in one sitting. (The most common definition is two to six shows in a row.) One self-pro-

The availability online of multiple episodes of television series can lead to a type of behavior known as binge-watching. Depression and obesity are two possible health consequences of such behavior.

fessed binge-watching addict, Michael Pollock, says that for him it was a way to escape from his life's challenges, fears, problems, and obstacles. "I used TV to distract myself from the shame, embarrassment and depression I felt about some irresponsible financial decisions and their resulting fallout," he says. "I used TV to avoid facing my fear of stepping out into the world more fully, connecting with others and pursuing the higher purpose to which my soul was calling. I used TV to fill the void of an otherwise empty life."[60]

According to a 2015 survey by TiVo, a subscription service that allows people to digitally record television shows, nine out of ten people in the United States binge-watch, with 66 percent of binge-watchers engaging in this activity via Netflix. Experts do not know how many people think they are addicted to binge-watching.

In fact, experts do not even agree on whether compulsive binge-watching should actually be classified as an addiction. However, when binge-watchers share their experiences, their stories sound a lot like those of addicts. For example, writer Jessica Beuker says:

> Two years ago I began watching the hit series *Breaking Bad*. The show had already aired its finale at the time, and had recently put the entire series up on Netflix. . . . I watched five seasons in five days, sixty-two hours of television in less than a week. . . . I didn't sleep. I didn't shower, but instead took baths so that I could bring my laptop into the bathroom to continue watching. If I needed a drink of water, I would carry my laptop with me to the fridge. Cooking would take time away from my *Breaking Bad* time, so instead I lived off pizza and cereal. In the rare chance that I pushed pause, I would be researching the characters and watching interviews with the actors.[61]

"I watched five seasons in five days, sixty-two hours of television in less than a week. . . . I didn't sleep. I didn't shower, but instead took baths so that I could bring my laptop into the bathroom to continue watching."[61]

—Jessica Beuker, who binge-watched the series *Breaking Bad*.

In the TiVo survey, 31 percent of respondents said they had lost sleep because they had difficulty limiting their watching; 37 percent said they had lost entire weekends to the activity. Experts also note that binge-watching can be accompanied by depression. Sometimes this depression is what drives binge-watching behavior. Other times it is a result of the separation anxiety that can occur once a binge is over. "Five short days after starting *Breaking Bad*, I finished," Beuker remembers, "I sat in my sweatpants in the middle of my bed, staring down at my computer screen, and I started crying. Not because the episode was particularly sad, but because the series that I had devoted my life to for the past five days was already over, and I couldn't help but feel a little empty."[62]

ADHD, Autism, and Gaming Addictions

Studies suggest that children with attention-deficit/hyperactivity disorder (ADHD) or autism might be more prone to becoming addicted to video games. ADHD is characterized by excessive activity and difficulties controlling one's behavior and paying attention, while autism involves impairments related to communication and social skills. One study from the University of Missouri in 2013 involved 150 boys both with and without these disorders; those with the disorders, especially autism, played video games more often and for longer periods of time than those without. Many researchers believe that this is because certain aspects of video games are especially appealing to boys with such disorders. For example, video games do not require one-on-one interactions with peers and they offer a certain degree of predictability.

However, a few studies suggest that playing video games might worsen the symptoms of ADHD. This was the finding of a study out of Iowa State University. One of its authors, psychology doctoral candidate Edward Swing, says:

> Parents might think that playing video games makes their child [with attention problems] more manageable or even helps them focus their attention, but that may be at the expense of their behavior in other situations. . . . [For example, by] spending so much time playing video games, some children may miss out on opportunities to develop sustained, focused attention that they need in school.

Iowa State University, "Video Game Playing Can Compound Kids' Existing Attention Problems Says ISU Study," February 23, 2012. http://archive.news.iastate.edu.

Antisocial Behavior

Experts caution that binge-watching can also contribute to obesity because it involves long hours of inactivity. Extended periods of sitting can also increase a person's chance of developing diabetes and heart disease. Poor eating habits during a binge can contribute to such health problems as well.

Some experts believe that compulsive binge-watching can also encourage people to be asocial. According to the entertainment research firm Marketcast, 98 percent of binge-watchers watch at home and 56 percent prefer to watch alone. This means that for a majority of bingers, time watching television is time not spent engaging with others. However, others point out that binge-watching can strengthen social relationships, because knowing about popular television shows can create bonds with coworkers, friends, and family members. As Pamela B. Rutledge, director of the Media Psychology Research Center, says, "Shows with fan followings are often shared at the time of viewing with friends and can be shared again online, increasing the social connection."[63]

The same point has been made in relation to addictions to uploading, downloading, and sharing digital files and to actively participating in online fan sites devoted to popular media, movie and television stars, and recording artists. These activities provide people with common knowledge that can reinforce social bonds. Moreover, the Internet provides ample opportunities for people to connect with one another through online communication. Still, sitting in front of a computer or other device for long hours is physically isolating, and experts say that for certain individuals, it can be very detrimental.

CHAPTER FIVE

Controlling Online Entertainment

Many of the concerns related to online entertainment are associated with the fact that the Internet is largely uncontrolled. This means that for the most part, anyone—even a child—can easily find pornographic videos or violent video games on the Internet, or simply view images that are highly disturbing and offensive. It also means that people are free to go online over and over again, possibly to the point of addiction, and to share their opinions anonymously without facing any consequences for doing so. In fact, even when there are laws against a particular online activity—such as pirating videos—the Internet's anonymity makes it hard to hold people accountable for their actions.

The Internet's freewheeling, uncontrolled nature has led many people to regard it as a contemporary Wild West, a place where anything goes. "In the Wild West, people worried about two main things: property rights and survival," notes Yatri Trivedi, an Internet and technology expert. "The Internet's not really different."[64] This has led some to argue that like the real Wild West of America's frontier history, the Internet should be tamed, at least in regard to making the Internet experience safer and better for certain types of users.

Illegal Copying

One of the greatest concerns among people who share their creative efforts online is that their work will be stolen by others, whether by copying and taking credit for it or by downloading it without paying for it and then sharing or selling it to others. There is no way to know just how often this occurs, because few people get caught or come forward to admit wrong-doing.

However, there is no doubt that it is relatively easy to steal online content. This is in part because of computer features that enable easy copying. "Today, technology covertly assists us [with taking things]: ctrl+C to copy images, prose, code, video and more, ctrl+V to paste," notes Rhodri Marsden, who writes on issues related to cybertechnology. "Driven by a combination of greed, confusion, ignorance, pressure, laziness and ambition, an increasing number of people are looking at stuff other people have done and thinking, 'Wow. That's really good. I'll pretend that I did it.'"[65]

> "Driven by a combination of greed, confusion, ignorance, pressure, laziness and ambition, an increasing number of people are looking at stuff other people have done and thinking, 'Wow. That's really good. I'll pretend that I did it.'"[65]
>
> —Rhodri Marsden, who writes on issues related to cybertechnology.

In regard to stealing video content—an act commonly known as pirating—thieves often rely on online file-sharing sites that do not care about the legality of the files being shared there. This was the case when a pirating group calling itself Hive-CM8 stole an advance DVD copy of the 2015 movie *The Hateful Eight* and uploaded it to a file-sharing site. During its first day on the site, the film was downloaded more than 200,000 times.

Copies of movies have also been stolen via hacking (whereby someone breaks into a computer system to steal its data) or by secretly recording a film while watching it in a theater and then using a program to improve the recording's quality and upload it to the Internet. However a movie is pirated, the more advance publicity it gets, the more likely it is to be illegally uploaded to the Internet. In addition, the more popular a movie is in theaters, the more often it will be illegally downloaded. For example, according to the piracy tracking firm Excipio, the top three movies that

The blockbuster film Furious 7, *with nearly 45 million illegal downloads, is one of the most frequently viewed pirated movies.*

were illegally downloaded in 2015 were all blockbusters: *Furious 7* (nearly 45 million downloads), *Avengers: Age of Ultron* (about 41.5 million downloads), and *Jurassic World* (about 37 million downloads).

The Excuse of Expense

People who steal content often justify their actions by saying that production companies have more than enough money to weather a few thefts. In fact, some argue that such companies are to blame for the pirating problem because they have made their products too expensive for many people to afford. Many of those who illegally download movies and television shows, for example, say that if they could afford to buy them they would. This logic angers honest people like gamer Danny Perez-Crouse. "In reality, it doesn't matter if something is too expensive or if the entity being stolen from has tons of money," he says. "If it isn't yours and you don't have the money to buy it, you can't have it. You're not entitled to something you may want, because it's out of your financial reach."[66]

Decreasing Motivation

When creative content is stolen, major corporations are not the only ones impacted—individuals and society as a whole are hurt too. This is because when people think it is easy to appropriate someone else's efforts without incurring any consequences, they become less motivated to produce their own works. Psychologist Shelley H. Carson explains why:

> Stealing the intellectual property of others decreases motivation to produce original material across the board in two ways. Even if you have . . . great ideas to share, your motivation to take the time and energy to do so is diminished if you can just purloin other work and pass it off as yours. Also, if someone else is going to take credit for your work without consequence to them, you will simply be less likely to produce further work and put it "out there" [on the Internet].

Shelley H. Carson, "Plagiarism and Its Effect on Creative Work," *Psychology Today*, October 16, 2010. www.psychologytoday.com.

Piracy in the gaming industry continues to grow, and experts predict that soon the amount of money that gamers are effectively stealing will be more than what they are spending on gaming. But there is evidence that movie piracy can be reduced simply by making it harder to pirate films than to watch them legally. For example, as Netflix has made it easier for subscribers to legally watch movies and television shows, piracy of such content has decreased.

Holding Back Content

Those who would like to see increased control over the Internet say that the people who run file-sharing sites need to be held more accountable, legally and financially, for the acts of piracy they enable. They also say that laws related to piracy and plagiarism need to be strengthened and more aggressively enforced.

But some take a more stark approach to protecting their creative works: not sharing them online at all. Of course, this prevents them from reaping any of the benefits that sometimes come from posting work online. Nonetheless, according to a survey released in May 2016 by the US Department of Commerce's Telecommunications and Information Administration, people are beginning to share less of themselves—their works, their opinions, their personal information (including financial data)—on the Internet. In fact, nearly half of all Internet users have cut back on activities related to providing personal material online, including making comments on public forums. Experts say this is because many people no longer trust the Internet to be a safe place to reveal details about themselves.

Anonymous Speech

Some website and application makers have implemented policies intended to keep the Internet and its users safe. Twitter, for example, suspends users who verbally abuse others; other forums, blogs, and comment sections have rules regarding what can be shared there, with moderators enforcing those rules. However, one issue with policing such speech is that there are often not enough moderators to keep up with the volume of material being shared, which makes the system ineffective. In addition, there are far fewer moderated areas of the Internet than unmoderated ones.

Another problem with policing online speech is that many argue that doing so imposes on the right to free speech. This issue has been raised as US politicians have proposed laws that would make Internet content providers responsible for policing speech on their websites. US courts have consistently upheld people's right to express themselves under the First Amendment of the Constitution, but lawmakers have tried to pass laws on the grounds that anonymous speech should not be protected. One such law was proposed in 2012 by the New York state legislature. It would have required administrators of New York–based websites to delete all

anonymous posts within forty-eight hours of their appearance, including those on "social networks, blog forums, message boards, or any other discussion site where people can hold conversations in the form of posted messages."[67] However, if an anonymous poster agreed to fully identify himself or herself within the forty-eight-hour period, the comment could remain.

The lawmakers said their aim was not to stifle speech but to keep people from attacking others anonymously. As assemblyman Jim Conte, cosponsor of the bill, explains: "With more and more people relying on social media and the Internet to communicate and gather information, it is imperative that the legislature put into place some type of safeguard to prevent people from using the Internet's cloak of anonymity to bully our children and make false accusations against local businesses and elected officials."[68]

Nonetheless, legal experts correctly noted that had this law passed, it would have been unconstitutional. Kurt Opsahl, an attorney with the Electronic Frontier Foundation, a digital rights group, says:

> The right to speak anonymously is part of the First Amendment and has been since the founding of this country. In fact, some of the founding documents of the country were originally written as part of the Federalist Papers, which some of our founding fathers wrote anonymously under pseudonyms. Since then, the Supreme Court has routinely held up the legality of speaking anonymously.[69]

International Issues

But even if such laws were constitutional, officials in the United States could not enforce them throughout the Internet. This is because the Internet is global, and people who do not live in the

United States are not subject to its laws. Therefore, a law about Internet content in the United States would not be applicable to people uploading content many countries away.

In addition, it would take the cooperation of international authorities to make even the smallest headway in controlling the Internet, whether regarding anonymous speech, content theft, or obscene or excessively violent images. There would also have to be safeguards in place to prevent criminals (whether individuals or websites or corporations) from avoiding the consequences of laws enacted in one location by simply fleeing to another.

Because of this, some have suggested that an international body or transnational entity be created to police the entirety of the Internet. Trivedi, for example, insists that "if regulation is a must, then there needs to be a world-wide agency or committee that sets rules"[70] that will protect the activities of legitimate Internet users while curbing the behavior of those who engage in wrongful activities. To this end, some government entities have tried to establish enforceable rules related to online content, particularly when it comes to protecting children from gaining access to entertainment that is only for adults. For example, in 2010 the European Union called on its member nations to work toward establishing ways to verify the ages of individuals accessing online content that might be harmful to minors.

As a result of this call to action, in 2014 the United Kingdom implemented legislation whereby Internet providers of pornographic content are required to have a system to verify that users are age eighteen or older. Proof of verification can include confirmation of credit card ownership (provided the card cannot be issued to anyone who is not over the age of eighteen), identification data from voter rolls, possession and ownership of an age-verified mobile phone, or any other proof of account ownership that requires a verification of age. Any Internet pornography provider who does not verify users' ages can be fined and/or have its site shut down.

Shutting Down Websites

However, the United Kingdom can control only those websites that are under its legal jurisdiction. It cannot fine or shut down a pornographic website based in Russia, for example. But sites can be difficult to shut down even when they originate from in-country: even US-based websites can be extremely difficult for US authorities to shut down, largely because it can take a long time to find those responsible for the site. Nonetheless, there have been successful efforts in this regard. For example, the US Department of Justice and the Department of Homeland Security have worked together to shut down thousands of websites associated with illegal child pornography. (This involves getting a judge to sign a warrant that allows federal agents to seize certain Internet do-

This agent for US Immigration and Customs Enforcement, along with his colleagues, works to shut down thousands of websites associated with child pornography.

mains and associated websites.) Similarly, federal agents have shut down websites that support piracy or illegally live-stream sporting events. For example, in February 2012 agents from the US Immigration and Customs Enforcement together with other agencies seized 307 websites that either live-streamed sports or sold fake NFL paraphernalia.

Because the process of shutting down a website can be complex, in cases where an Internet offense is minor the US government often prefers to simply ask an Internet provider to remove problematic website content. For example, Google routinely receives requests from US law enforcement agencies and courts to remove content from its web properties, which include YouTube and a blog platform. In one case, a law enforcement group asked Google to take down fourteen hundred YouTube videos it felt constituted harassment. In another, a law enforcement agency requested that a blog be removed because it made defamatory statements about an official with the agency. Google rejected these requests, however, saying it was unwilling to remove entertainment-related content when no law had been broken.

Filters

Given the difficulties associated with trying to remove troublesome Internet content, some people argue that it is more effective to use filters to prevent Internet users from encountering material they do not want to see. Library computers, for example, typically contain software that prevents them from accessing sites that are inappropriate for young people, and individuals who struggle with Internet addictions can install software on their computers that will block their access to certain websites they know are problematic for them.

In addition to filters that block specific websites, some filters recognize strings of characters as being related to undesirable content. Most often these are words related to pornography, hate speech, or graphic violence. When such words are found on a website, the system will not allow access to it even if the site is not on its pre-established list of sites to block.

Fighting for Better Laws

In January 2013 Virginia attorney Andaleeb Geloo found out that people were saying vile things about her on a community website called FairfaxUnderground. The remarks came after a client had given Geloo a good review about the way she had handled his case. Some of the responses said that the client and Geloo should both die in a horrific car crash. Others included vulgar sexual comments about Geloo and/or vicious attacks on aspects of her appearance. Many said she was a horrible lawyer and should be disbarred.

Geloo wanted to sue ten of the worst offenders, but they had all posted anonymously. At the time, the law gave her only a year to sue someone for defamation of character. She worked hard to try to identify those who had written about her (known in the law as "John Does"). However, the process of doing so was long and complicated, and by the time she identified one of them, her time to prosecute under the law had run out. Consequently, Geloo turned her attention to changing the law. She succeeded in 2015, when the Virginia state legislature passed a bill that allows a reasonable amount of extra time to be spent on a defamation lawsuit if the offender is a John Doe, specifically to give the litigant a better chance of unmasking the anonymous person.

However, content filters can unintentionally exclude desirable or acceptable material, which some regard as problematic. According to the Electronic Privacy Information Center, "The process is fraught with error and there are rarely effective means to check whether a site is blocked inappropriately, to correct the problem, to override the blocking, or to appeal the multitude of incorrect decisions made by blocking technology companies."[71] Other flaws in Internet blocking systems, according to critics, include underblocking, overblocking, and the fact that the creators of blocking systems are the ones that determine what is and is not appropriate content.

Filters can also lull people into believing they have taken care of a problem once and for all. For example, parents who use software to block their home computers' access to online pornography sites might think they no longer need to worry about their children gaining access to such sites. But in reality their children could just as easily access pornography via a mobile device or a friend's personal computer—and tech-savvy kids can often figure out ways around filters, especially since such software is designed to be installed by adults with limited computer experience. As Internet data expert Mona Chalabi says, "A filter has to be simple enough for technologically feeble adults but difficult enough to stop a tech-savvy 17-year-old working out how to bypass it. Arguably, no such filter exists."[72]

Therefore many experts believe it is better for parents to educate young people about the problems associated with pornography than to rely on filters to block porn sites—and to educate

A worker at a public library helps a patron use a computer to check his e-mail. Libraries try to limit access to pornography with software that either blocks specific websites or recognizes strings of characters associated with undesirable content.

parents about not only the nature of the Internet but the behavior of young people. This is the view of Jerry Barnett, founder of an anti-censorship group called Sex & Censorship. He advocates "parental education and sex education for children"[73] because he believes it is ridiculous to assume that young people can avoid sexually explicit material on the Internet until they are over eighteen—especially since during adolescence they will likely try to seek it out.

A Block on Freedom

There are also those who argue that blocking access to pornographic yet legal Internet content, even for the purpose of keeping minors from viewing adults-only material, is the first step down a slippery slope. That is, they fear that censoring one type of content will soon lead to censoring others, thereby eroding people's rights. In this way, some speculate, Western countries that value freedom of thought and expression will become like countries that censor many types of content.

This is the case, for example, with China. Its government uses search-engine filters to prevent its citizens from accessing information online that its officials deem inappropriate—including subjects related to sensitive political issues. As a result, typing words like "persecution," "Tibetan independence," or "democracy movements" into a search engine results in the message, "Page cannot be displayed."[74]

> "Content-based censorship of America's entertainment industry must be avoided at all costs."[75]
>
> —Political writer Tom Rogan.

Many Americans find the prospect that such an extreme degree of censorship might one day occur in the United States to be chilling. This is why political writer Tom Rogan speaks for many when he says, "Content-based censorship of America's entertainment industry must be avoided at all costs." He thinks that restricting entertainment-related content, activities, and speech is a strike against democracy. "While individually, we might not always agree with its products," he says, "our entertainment industry is nonetheless at the heart of what America is all about."[75]

SOURCE NOTES

Introduction: The Nature of Online Entertainment

1. Lana Gorlinski, "Confessions of a Teenage Internet Addict," *Huffington Post*, July 2, 2013. www.huffingtonpost.com.
2. Marcus Wohlsen, "The Internet Is Officially More Popular than Cable in the U.S.," *Wired*, August 15, 2014. www.wired.com.
3. PwC, "Beyond Digital: Empowered Consumers Seek Out Tailored, Inspiring Content Experiences That Transcend Platforms and Can Be Shared," *Global Entertainment and Media Outlook, 2015–2019*. www.pwc.com.
4. Dave Court et al., "We All Know Movie Piracy Is Wrong. So Why Do We Do It?," *Lifehacker*, August 20, 2015. www.lifehacker.com.au.

Chapter One: How the Internet Has Affected Entertainment Providers

5. Jeff Price, "Why Everyone but the Artist and the Music Fan Is Doomed," *TuneCore* (blog), November 21, 2011. www.tunecore.com.
6. Price, "Why Everyone but the Artist and the Music Fan Is Doomed."
7. Clint Rainey, "I Was Internet-Famous," *New York*, December 2, 2015. http://nymag.com.
8. Rainey, "I Was Internet-Famous."
9. Seija Rankin, "EL James Did a Twitter Q&A and It Was a Giant Disaster," *EOnline*, June 29, 2015. www.eonline.com.
10. Quoted in Rachel Randall, "How Hugh Howey Turned His Self-Published Story 'Wool' into a Success (& a Book Deal)," *Writers Digest*, January 23, 2014. www.writersdigest.com.
11. Quoted in Alexandra Alter, "The Weird World of Fan Fiction," *Wall Street Journal*, June 14, 2012. www.wsj.com.
12. Quoted in T'Bonz, "Axanar's Peters Talks About Lawsuit," *Trek Today*, February 1, 2016. www.trektoday.com.
13. Matt Saccaro, "Do We Need a New Definition of Plagiarism?," *Daily Dot*, August 1, 2014. www.dailydot.com.
14. Quoted in Alter, "The Weird World of Fan Fiction."
15. Quoted in Alter, "The Weird World of Fan Fiction."

16. Quoted in Rhodri Marsden, "The Big Steal: Rise of the Plagiarist in the Digital Age," *Guardian* (Manchester), March 21, 2014. www.theguardian.com.
17. J.A. Konrath, "The New Role of Gatekeepers," *J.A. Konrath* (blog), February 10, 2014. http://jakonrath.blogspot.com.

Chapter Two: Are Video Games Entertaining or Harmful?

18. Quoted in Press Association, "Cybercriminals 'Often Start Out with Minor Thefts in Online Games,'" *Guardian* (Manchester), February 7, 2015. www.theguardian.com.
19. Tom Hoggins, "Grand Theft Auto V Is Designed Deliberately to Degrade Women," *Telegraph* (London), October 4, 2013. www.telegraph.co.uk.
20. Hoggins, "Grand Theft Auto V Is Designed Deliberately to Degrade Women."
21. Matthew Johnson, "Encountering Racist and Sexist Content Online," MediaSmarts, June 19, 2014. http://mediasmarts.ca.
22. Quoted in Robert Purchese, "Misogyny, Racism and Homophobia: Where Do Video Games Stand?," *Eurogamer*, March 21, 2014. www.eurogamer.net.
23. Erik Kain, "Do Games Like 'Grand Theft Auto V' Cause Real-World Violence?," *Forbes*, September 18, 2013. www.forbes.com.
24. Quoted in Mike Jaccarino, "'Training Simulation': Mass Killers Often Share Obsession with Violent Video Games," Fox News, September 12, 2013. www.foxnews.com.
25. Quoted in Helen Pidd, "Anders Breivik 'Trained for Shooting Attacks by Playing Call of Duty,'" *Guardian* (Manchester), April 19, 2012. www.theguardian.com.
26. Paul Tassi, "The Idiocy of Blaming Video Games for the Norway Massacre," *Forbes*, April 19, 2012. www.forbes.com.
27. Dave Grossman, Phi Kappa Phi National Forum, Fall 2000. www.killology.com/print/print_teachkid.htm.
28. Quoted in Jeff Grabmeier, "Video Games Can Teach How to Shoot Guns More Accurately and Aim for the Head," Ohio State University Research Communications, April 30, 2012. http://researchnews.osu.edu.
29. Quoted in American Psychological Association, "APA Review Confirms Link Between Playing Violent Video Games and Aggression," August 13, 2015. www.apa.org.
30. Quoted in Jaccarino, "'Training Simulation.'"

31. Quoted in Dave Larsen, "Study: Violent Video Games Increase Aggression," *Dayton Daily News*, February 1, 2013. www.daytondaily news.com.

32. Kain, "Do Games Like 'Grand Theft Auto V' Cause Real-World Violence?"

Chapter Three: Concerns About Online Pornography

33. Quoted in Ross Benes, "Porn: The Hidden Engine That Drives Innovation in Tech," *Business Insider*, July 5, 2013. www.business insider.com.

34. Paul Rudo, "Ten Indispensable Technologies Built by the Pornography Industry," Enterprise Features, June 5, 2011. www.enterprise features.com.

35. Quoted in David L. Hudson Jr., "Pornography and Obscenity," First Amendment Center, September 13, 2002. www.firstamendment center.org.

36. Quoted in Ben Russell, "Federal Agents Arrest More than a Dozen in Internet Child Pornography Ring," *NBC Dallas-Fort Worth News*, March 19, 2014. www.nbcdfw.com.

37. Quoted in David Segal, "Does Porn Hurt Children?," *New York Times*, March 3, 2014. www.nytimes.com.

38. Quoted in Segal, "Does Porn Hurt Children?"

39. Quoted in Segal, "Does Porn Hurt Children?"

40. Quoted in Pam Horne, "Teens Engaged in Sexting, Cyber Bullying Face Potential Felony Charges," *Williamson (Franklin, TN) Herald*, February 23, 2014. www.williamsonherald.com.

41. News Release, "Teens Arrested After Tweeting Video of Group Sex," Justice News Flash, April 2, 2015. www.justicenewsflash.com.

42. Quoted in Andrea Weckerle, "Antibullying Advocate and Sexting Victim Allyson Pereira Shares Her Story," CiviliNation, October 25, 2011. www.civilination.org.

43. Quoted in Weckerle, "Antibullying Advocate and Sexting Victim Allyson Pereira Shares Her Story."

44. Raychelle Cassada Lohmann, "The Dangers of Teen Sexting," *Psychology Today*, July 20, 2012. www.psychologytoday.com.

45. Quoted in Belinda Goldsmith, "Safe 'Sexting'? No Such Thing, Teens Warned," *Reuters*, May 4, 2009. www.reuters.com.

46. Syras Derksen, "Negative Effects of Pornography," *Dr. Syras Derksen & Associates* (blog), October 14, 2013. www.drsyrasderksen .com.

47. Quoted in American Osteopathic Association press release, "Top Five Warning Signs of Internet Pornography Addiction," October 27, 2014. www.osteopathic.org.

Chapter Four: When Online Entertainment Becomes Addictive

48. Center for Internet Addiction, "FAQs: What Is Internet Addiction Disorder?" http://netaddiction.com.
49. DSM-5, "Internet Gaming Disorder," American Psychiatric Association, May 2013. www.dsm5.org.
50. Center for Internet Addiction, "Internet Gaming Disorder." http://netaddiction.com.
51. Quoted in Tom Meltzer, "I Was a Games Addict," *Guardian* (Manchester), March 11, 2011. www.theguardian.com.
52. Quoted in Meltzer, "I Was a Games Addict."
53. Meltzer, "I Was a Games Addict."
54. Quoted in Meltzer, "I Was a Games Addict."
55. Quoted in Tamara Lush, "At War with World of Warcraft: An Addict Tells His Story," *Guardian* (Manchester), August 29, 2011. www.theguardian.com.
56. Quoted in Ned Hepburn, "Life in the Age of Internet Addiction," *Week*, January 24, 2013. http://theweek.com.
57. Quoted in Ruth Lythe, "The Cynical Websites Using Pictures of Kittens and Cupcakes to Lure Women into Debt and Despair: How to Turn a Middle-Class Woman into an Online Gambling Addict," *Daily Mail* (London), April 23, 2014. www.dailymail.co.uk.
58. Quoted in Lythe, "The Cynical Websites Using Pictures of Kittens and Cupcakes to Lure Women into Debt and Despair."
59. Quoted in Lythe, "The Cynical Websites Using Pictures of Kittens and Cupcakes to Lure Women into Debt and Despair."
60. Michael Pollock, "How I Overcame TV Addiction, Reclaimed My Life, and Gained Two Months per Year," *Michael D. Pollock* (blog). www.michaeldpollock.com.
61. Jessica Beuker, "How Binge-Watching Is Ruining Television and Making You Depressed," *Plaid Zebra*, March 12, 2016. www.theplaidzebra.com.
62. Beuker, "How Binge-Watching Is Ruining Television and Making You Depressed."
63. Pamela B. Rutledge, "Binge Viewing Redefines TV Watching," *Psychology Today*, April 12, 2014. www.psychologytoday.com.

Chapter Five: Controlling Online Entertainment

64. Yatri Trivedi, "Geek Rants: Why the Internet Is Like the Wild West," How-To Geek, May 5, 2011. www.howtogeek.com.

65. Rhodri Marsden, "The Big Steal: Rise of the Plagiarist in the Digital Age," *Guardian* (Manchester), March 21, 2014. www.theguardian.com.

66. Danny Perez-Crouse, "Piracy Can't Be Justified," *Advocate*, February 20, 2014. www.advocate-online.net.

67. Quoted in Amanda Holpuch, "New York Lawmakers Propose Bill to Ban Anonymous Online Speech," *Guardian* (Manchester), May 23, 2012. www.theguardian.com.

68. Quoted in Alex Fitzpatrick, "Lawmakers Call for an End to Internet Anonymity," Mashable, May 23, 2012. http://mashable.com.

69. Electronic Privacy Information Center, "Censorware: A Post-CDA Solution?," October 1, 2002. https://epic.org.

70. Trivedi, "Geek Rants."

71. Electronic Privacy Information Center, "Censorware: A Post-CDA Solution?"

72. Mona Chalabi, "Porn Filters: 12 Reasons Why They Won't Work (and 3 Reasons Why They Might)," *Guardian* (Manchester), August 8, 2013. www.theguardian.com.

73. Quoted in Liat Clark, "Regulator Wants UK Law to Protect Under-18s from Porn," *Wired UK*, March 28, 2014. www.wired.co.uk.

74. Paul Weisman and *USA Today*, "Cracking the 'Great Wall' of Chinese Censorship," ABC News. http://abcnews.go.com.

75. Tom Rogan, "America, Do Not Censor Our Entertainment," *Huffington Post*, January 18, 2013. www.huffingtonpost.com.

ORGANIZATIONS TO CONTACT

Center for Internet Addiction
PO Box 72
Bradford, PA 16701
phone: (814) 451-2405
website: www.netaddiction.com

The Center for Internet Addiction offers counseling for problematic Internet use and related issues. Its website provides information on issues such as compulsive web surfing and online gambling.

Center for Internet and Technology Addiction
17 S. Highland St.
West Hartford, CT 06119
phone: (860) 561-8727
e-mail: drdave@virtual-addiction.com
website: www.virtual-addiction.com

The Center for Internet and Technology Addiction provides counseling, information, and resources related to online addictions. Its website offers articles, news releases, and videos related to these addictions.

Common Sense Media
650 Townsend, Suite 435
San Francisco, CA 94103
phone: (415) 863-0600
website: http://commonsensemedia.org

Common Sense Media provides information and advice related to media and technology. The organization's aim is to help people make smart choices when they go online. It also works with teachers and others to create educational programs related to digital safety issues, including sexting.

Entertainment Software Association (ESA)
575 Seventh St. NW, Suite 300
Washington, DC 20004
e-mail: esa@theesa.com
website: www.theesa.com

A trade association, the ESA represents companies that publish and market video games and has been involved in legal efforts to fight the censorship of games and the restriction of their sales to minors.

Fight the New Drug
phone: (385) 313-8629
website: www.fightthenewdrug.org

Fight the New Drug's mission is to raise awareness on the harmful effects of pornography. Its website contains information and resources aimed at helping teenagers and adults deal with the effects of pornography use.

Morality in Media
1100 G St. NW #1030
Washington, DC 20005
phone: (202) 393-7245
website: moralityinmedia.org
website: http://pornharms.com
Morality in Media is a national nonprofit organization dedicated to opposing online obscenity and indecency through public education and application of the law. Its companion website, Porn Harms, contains news and resources specific to online pornography.

On-Line Gamers Anonymous (OGA)
PO Box 67
Osceola, WI 54020
phone: (612) 245-1115
website: www.olganon.org

The OGA is a fellowship group for compulsive gamers that also offers support for the loved ones of people suffering from a gaming addiction.

Books

Dave Grossman and Gloria DeGaetano, *Stop Teaching Our Kids to Kill*. New York: Harmony, 2014.

Samuel McQuade et al., *Internet Addiction and Online Gaming*. New York: Chelsea House, 2012.

Vanessa Rogers, *Educating Young People About Pornography*. London: Kingsley, 2016.

Bernadette H. Schell, *Internet Censorship: A Reference Handbook*. Santa Barbara, CA: ABC-CLIO, 2014.

Bernadette H. Schell, *Online Health and Safety: From Cyberbullying to Internet Addiction*. Westport, CT: Greenwood, 2016.

Internet Sources

Center for Problem Policing, "Effects of Child Pornography," 2016. www.popcenter.org/problems/child_pornography/2.

Maria Konnikova, "Is Internet Addiction a Real Thing?," *New Yorker*, November 26, 2014. http://www.newyorker.com/science /maria-konnikova/internet-addiction-real-thing.

Reuters, "How Network TV Figured Out Binge-Watching," *Fortune*, March 11, 2016. http://fortune.com/2016/03/11/netflix -changing-game-network-tv.

Websites

On-Line Gamers Anonymous (www.olganon.org/home). A support group and educational resource for those addicted to online video games.

Video Game Addiction (www.video-game-addiction.org). This site defines gaming addiction; lists the most addicting games currently available; and offers resources for those who are concerned they or someone they know has a gaming addiction.

Your Brain on Porn (www.yourbrainonporn.com). This site, steeped in scientific sources, shows the negative impacts of viewing pornography on both male and female brains.

INDEX

PICTURE CREDITS

Cover: Shutterstock/Vectomart

6: Mactrunk/Depositphotos

10: Yonhap News/YNA/Newscom

12: Allen Eyestone/ZUMA Press/Newscom

16: Paramount Pictures/Photofest

20: Ale Ventura/Altopress/Newscom

22: Corbis/Splash News/Newscom

27: Billy Suratt/UPI Photo Service/Newscom

33: Joe Burbank/MCT/Newscom

37: AltoPress/Maxppp

41: Depositphotos

45: MBR/KRT/Newscom

49: Associated Press

51: Depositphotos

57: Universal Pictures/Photofest

62: Associated Press

65: Mark Avery/ZUMA Press/Newscom

ABOUT THE AUTHOR

Patricia D. Netzley is the author of dozens of books for children, teens, and adults. She also teaches writing and is a member of the Society of Children's Book Writers and Illustrators (SCBWI).